Stream and Create

Stream and Create

Big Daddy Dakota 96.67

BIGDADDY
DAKOTA 96.67

First Printing, 2025

Contents

1

Understanding Membership Platforms

The Rise of Membership-Based Models

The emergence of membership-based models has fundamentally transformed the landscape of content creation and consumption. Platforms like OnlyFans, Patreon, and Fansly have empowered creators to directly monetize their work, fostering a vibrant community of dedicated fans willing to support their favorite artists, educators, and entertainers. This shift not only provides a sustainable income for creators but also facilitates a more intimate connection between them and their audience. As a result, the rise of these models represents an exciting opportunity for content creators to explore innovative ways to engage with their supporters while delivering unique experiences that cater to their interests.

In the realm of video content production, membership platforms have opened the door to diverse storytelling possibilities. Creators can now craft exclusive video content that resonates deeply with their audience, offering behind-the-scenes insights, tutorials, or personalized messages that traditional platforms couldn't accommodate. This level of engagement not only enhances the viewing experience but also fosters a sense of belonging among subscribers, who feel valued for their support. Embracing this model allows creators to experiment with different formats, styles, and themes, ultimately leading to richer and more fulfilling content that keeps members coming back for more.

Writing engaging blog posts for subscription models has become an essential tool for creators looking to deepen their connection with their audience. By sharing insights, experiences, and behind-the-scenes stories, content creators can create a narrative that complements their video productions. These blog posts serve as a powerful means of storytelling, allowing fans to understand the creative process while also providing valuable information that enhances their overall experience. The key is to maintain a conversational tone that invites readers to engage, comment, and share their thoughts, further strengthening the community dynamic.

Additionally, interactive content development is crucial in maintaining member engagement. Creators can leverage polls, quizzes, and live Q&A sessions to foster a sense of community and encourage active participation. This dynamic approach not only keeps content fresh and exciting but also allows fans to play an integral role in shaping the content they consume. By encouraging user-generated content, creators can cultivate a sense of ownership among their members, making them feel like active participants in the creative journey rather than mere spectators.

In conclusion, the rise of membership-based models presents an incredible opportunity for creators to thrive in a rapidly evolving digital landscape. By focusing on video content production, engaging writing, and interactive strategies, content creators can build strong, lasting relationships with their audience. Embracing these models means not just creating content but also fostering a community where members feel connected, valued, and excited to be part of the journey. As you navigate this vibrant ecosystem, remember that your creativity and authenticity are your greatest assets in achieving membership success.

Key Features of Successful Membership Sites

Successful membership sites share several key features that can significantly enhance user engagement and retention, especially for content creators on platforms like OnlyFans, Patreon, and Fansly. First and foremost, a clear value proposition is essential. Members need to understand what unique benefits they gain from subscribing. This could be exclusive video content, behind-the-scenes access, or personal interaction opportunities. By communicating your value proposition effectively, you establish a strong reason for potential members to join and stay connected.

Another critical feature is the consistency of content delivery. Successful membership sites thrive on a regular schedule that keeps members coming back for more. Whether it's weekly video releases, monthly live Q&A sessions, or daily posts, maintaining a consistent rhythm fosters anticipation and loyalty. Content creators should leverage tools and platforms that allow for easy scheduling and automation, ensuring that even during busy times, members receive the content they expect.

Engagement through community-building is also vital. Creating a sense of belonging among members encourages interaction and loyalty. Utilize forums, chat groups, or live streams to facilitate connections between members. This not only enhances the overall experience but also motivates members to participate actively. By fostering a supportive community, you create an environment where members feel valued and involved, which can lead to increased retention rates.

Interactive content is another hallmark of successful membership platforms. Incorporating polls, quizzes, or live feedback sessions keeps members engaged and invested in the content. This approach allows you to adapt your offerings based on member preferences, making them feel heard and valued. Additionally, by involving members in the creative process, you can generate user-generated content that enriches the community and presents fresh perspectives.

Lastly, effective marketing strategies are crucial for promoting membership content and retaining subscribers. Utilizing social media, email marketing, and collaborations with other creators can significantly expand your reach. Consistently sharing highlights of your exclusive content can entice new members while keeping current ones informed and excited about upcoming offerings. By implementing these strategies, you not only attract a wider audience but also cultivate a dedicated member base, ensuring the long-term success of your membership platform.

Identifying Your Target Audience

Identifying your target audience is a crucial step for any content creator, especially those operating on membership platforms like OnlyFans, Patreon, and Fansly. Understanding who your audience is will inform the type of content you create, how you engage with them, and ultimately, how you can build a loyal community around your brand. Start by analyzing the demographics of your current subscribers or followers. Consider their age, gender, location, and interests. This information will help you tailor your content to meet their preferences and expectations, making them feel valued and understood.

Next, delve deeper into the psychographics of your audience. What are their passions, hobbies, and challenges? By tapping into their desires and pain points, you can create more meaningful and relevant content. For instance, if you notice that your subscribers are interested in fitness, incorporating workout videos or health tips can greatly increase engagement. Remember, your goal is to create a connection that resonates with your audience on a personal level, which will encourage them to stay subscribed and engaged with your content.

Engaging with your audience directly can also provide valuable insights into their preferences. Utilize polls, surveys, or Q&A sessions to gather feedback about the type of content they want to see. This not only helps you generate ideas but also makes your audience feel actively involved in the content creation process. Their input can guide you in developing interactive content that fosters community engagement, such as live streams or collaborative projects. Listening to your audience's voices will strengthen their connection to you and your brand.

Analyzing your competitors can also shed light on your target audience. Look at similar creators in your niche and assess their engagement levels, content types, and audience interactions. This can provide a clearer picture of what works and what doesn't, enabling you to carve out your unique space in the market. By understanding the dynamics of the audience that engages with your competitors, you can refine your approach and differentiate your offerings, ensuring that you attract your ideal subscribers.

Finally, as you identify your target audience, remember that it's not a one-time process. Audiences evolve, and so do their interests. Regularly revisit your audience analysis to stay current with their changing preferences. This practice will not only help you remain relevant but also encourage long-term loyalty among your subscribers. By continuously adapting and responding to your audience's needs, you'll foster a thriving community that supports your membership platform and celebrates your creative endeavors.

2

Creating Compelling Video Content

Essential Video Production Techniques

Understanding essential video production techniques is crucial for content creators looking to thrive on membership platforms like OnlyFans, Patreon, and Fansly. The quality of your video content directly impacts your ability to engage and retain subscribers, making it vital to invest time in mastering various production elements. From lighting and sound to editing and storytelling, each aspect plays a significant role in creating compelling videos that resonate with your audience. By honing these skills, you can enhance your content's appeal, ensuring your subscribers feel valued and connected to your brand.

Lighting is one of the first and most important elements to consider when producing video content. Good lighting not only improves the visual quality of your videos but also helps convey the right mood and atmosphere. Natural light can be a great option, but investing in softbox lights or ring lights can provide consistency, especially for indoor shoots. Experiment with different lighting setups to see how they affect your presentation. Remember, well-lit videos can make even the simplest content feel professional and engaging, encouraging viewers to stay longer and interact more with your offerings.

Sound quality is another critical element that often gets overlooked. Poor audio can distract viewers and detract from your message, no matter how visually stunning your video may be. Using an external microphone can significantly improve your sound quality compared to built-in camera mics. Additionally, pay attention to background noise and consider using soundproofing techniques or filming in quiet environments. Good sound not only enhances the viewer's experience but also makes your content feel more polished and credible, fostering trust in your community.

Editing is where your raw footage transforms into a cohesive story. Utilizing editing software allows you to cut out mistakes, add transitions, and incorporate graphics or text that enhance your narrative. Focus on pacing; a well-edited video keeps viewers engaged and encourages them to consume your content all the way through. Don't shy away from learning new editing techniques—there are countless tutorials available that can help you refine your skills. With practice, you'll find your unique style, which can further distinguish your content in the crowded membership landscape.

Finally, remember that storytelling is at the heart of successful video production. Crafting a compelling narrative can draw viewers in and keep them invested in your content. Whether you're sharing personal anecdotes, tutorials, or behind-the-scenes glimpses, think about how you can weave a story that resonates with your audience. Engaging narratives not only entertain but also foster a sense of community among your subscribers. As you develop your video production techniques, keep your audience's interests in mind, and always aim to create content that inspires, educates, and entertains. By mastering these essential techniques, you'll be well on your way to building a loyal and engaged membership community.

Equipment You Need for High-Quality Videos

When embarking on your journey to create high-quality videos for membership platforms like OnlyFans, Patreon, and Fansly, having the right equipment is essential. You don't need a massive budget to get started, but investing in some key tools can significantly enhance the quality of your content. Start with a reliable camera that fits your needs. While smartphones with good cameras can work wonders, consider upgrading to a DSLR or mirrorless camera for professional-grade video. The clarity and depth they provide will elevate your work, helping you stand out in a crowded space.

Lighting is just as crucial as the camera itself. Natural light is fantastic, but it can be inconsistent. Invest in softbox lights or ring lights to ensure your videos are well-lit, regardless of the time of day. Proper lighting not only enhances visual appeal but also creates an inviting atmosphere for your audience. This attention to detail will make your content feel more polished and engaging, encouraging viewers to subscribe and stay tuned for future releases.

Audio quality often gets overlooked, yet it plays a pivotal role in how your videos are received. Poor audio can detract from even the most visually stunning content. Consider using an external microphone to capture clear sound. Lavalier mics are great for close-up shots, while shotgun mics work well for more dynamic environments. Investing in good audio equipment will ensure that your messages are heard loud and clear, fostering a stronger connection with your audience.

Editing software is another essential piece of your production toolkit. While there are free options available, investing in more advanced software can provide you with the tools necessary for seamless editing. Programs such as Adobe Premiere Pro or Final Cut Pro offer a range of features that allow for creative expression and professional finishing touches. A well-edited video not only keeps your audience engaged but also enhances your credibility as a creator, making them more likely to support your work.

Finally, don't forget about the importance of a stable setup. Whether you're shooting at home or on location, a tripod or gimbal will help eliminate shaky footage, providing a more professional look. Stability in your videos communicates reliability and quality to your audience, making them more likely to engage with your content. By equipping yourself with these essential tools, you'll be well on your way to creating high-quality videos that resonate with your membership community and keep them coming back for more.

Editing Tips to Enhance Your Content

Editing is a crucial stage in the content creation process that can significantly elevate the quality of your work. For creators on membership platforms like OnlyFans, Patreon, and Fansly, the editing phase is not just about correcting mistakes; it's an opportunity to refine your message and engage your audience more effectively. Begin by reviewing your content with fresh eyes. Take a break after finishing your first draft, then return to it to identify areas for improvement. This distance will help you see your work more objectively, making it easier to spot inconsistencies and areas that need enhancement.

Focus on clarity and coherence in your content. Whether you're producing videos, writing blog posts, or developing podcasts, ensure your ideas flow logically from one point to the next. Use simple language and avoid jargon unless it's specific to your niche and your audience is familiar with it. Short sentences and paragraphs can enhance readability, especially for online content. Consider using bullet points or numbered lists to break down complex information, making it easier for your audience to digest and engage with your material.

Incorporating feedback from trusted peers or members of your community can also be invaluable. Sharing your content with fellow creators or a select group of loyal fans can provide insights that might not have crossed your mind. Constructive criticism can highlight strengths you may not recognize and pinpoint weaknesses that could undermine your message. Embrace this feedback as a gift that will help you fine-tune your content and make it even more appealing to your audience.

Another essential aspect of editing is the visual and auditory elements of your content. For video creators, this means reviewing your footage for pacing, transitions, and overall aesthetics. Ensure that visuals are engaging and support your narrative. For podcasts, focus on sound quality and clarity, removing any distracting background noise. Adding music or sound effects can enhance the listening experience, but be careful not to overwhelm your main content. Visual and auditory elements should complement your message, enhancing the overall experience for your audience.

Finally, don't forget to optimize your content for search engines and social media platforms. Use relevant keywords naturally throughout your content to enhance discoverability. This is particularly important for blog posts and video descriptions. Create captivating titles and thumbnails that entice potential viewers or readers. Editing is not just about polishing what you have; it's also about maximizing the reach and impact of your content. By following these editing tips, you can create compelling, high-quality material that resonates with your audience and encourages them to stay engaged with your membership offerings.

3

Engaging Blog Posts for Members

Crafting Titles That Capture Attention

Crafting compelling titles is essential for drawing in your audience and keeping them engaged with your content. Whether you're an OnlyFans model, Patreon user, or content creator on various platforms, the title serves as your first impression. It's the gateway that invites potential subscribers to explore further. To create titles that truly capture attention, focus on clarity, creativity, and a hint of intrigue. Clear titles let your audience know what to expect, while creative phrasing and an element of mystery can spark curiosity and encourage clicks.

Utilizing strong keywords relevant to your niche is another effective strategy. By incorporating terms that resonate with your audience's interests, you not only enhance your SEO but also ensure your titles speak directly to your target demographic. For instance, if you specialize in video content production, including keywords such as "exclusive," "behind-the-scenes," or "insider tips" can elevate your title's appeal. Think about what your subscribers are searching for and make sure your titles align with those interests, thus increasing the likelihood of engagement.

Engagement doesn't end with your title; it begins there. A captivating title sets the tone for the entire piece of content, whether it's a video, podcast, or blog post. Aim for titles that evoke emotions or provoke thought. Phrasing like "Unlock the Secrets to Successful Live Streaming" or "Discover the Hidden Gems of Membership Content" not only informs but also inspires action. This approach nurtures a sense of excitement and anticipation, making your audience more likely to commit time to your content.

Experimentation is key in developing titles that resonate with your audience. Don't hesitate to try different styles and formats. A/B testing can be an excellent method for gauging which titles perform best. Monitor engagement metrics closely—likes, shares, and comments can provide invaluable feedback. If one title consistently draws in more viewers, analyze its elements and consider how you can replicate that success in future titles. Your audience's preferences can evolve, so staying adaptable is crucial for long-term success.

Ultimately, crafting titles that capture attention is an art that combines strategy, creativity, and a deep understanding of your audience. Embrace the process and view it as an opportunity to connect with your subscribers on a deeper level. As you refine your title-writing skills, remember that each title is a chance to showcase your unique voice and offer something valuable to your community. With practice and perseverance, you'll find the perfect balance of attention-grabbing and informative titles that elevate your content and drive membership success.

Structuring Your Posts for Maximum Impact

Structuring your posts effectively is crucial for capturing the attention of your audience and maximizing engagement on membership platforms. Start with a compelling headline that not only grabs interest but also clearly articulates the value your content offers. Whether you're sharing a new video, an exclusive blog post, or a live stream event, your title should promise something valuable to your subscribers. This approach not only entices your audience to click but also sets the expectation for what they'll gain from your content.

Once you have their attention, the introduction of your post should engage readers immediately. Share a personal story, a surprising fact, or a question that resonates with your audience's interests. This initial hook is vital for creating a connection and encouraging further reading. Remember, your audience seeks authenticity and relatability; by being genuine in your approach, you reinforce their reasons for subscribing to your content. This establishes a rapport that can lead to increased loyalty and engagement.

After capturing interest, structure the body of your post in a way that is easy to digest. Use short paragraphs, bullet points, and subheadings to break down information and make it more accessible. Visual elements, such as images or videos, can also enhance understanding and retention of your message. Ensure that each section flows logically into the next, maintaining a clear narrative or argument throughout. This clarity will help your audience navigate through your content effortlessly, keeping them engaged and eager for more.

Incorporate interactive elements into your posts to foster engagement. Ask questions that prompt responses, create polls, or encourage comments and discussions. This not only allows your audience to feel involved but also gives you valuable feedback on what they enjoy or want more of. Engaging your community in this way transforms your content from a one-sided delivery into a two-way conversation, enhancing the sense of belonging that is essential for membership success.

Finally, conclude your posts with a strong call to action that encourages your audience to take the next step, whether it's subscribing, sharing, or engaging further with your content. Reinforce the benefits they will gain by taking action and express gratitude for their support. A well-structured post not only informs but also inspires your audience, turning casual viewers into committed members. By applying these strategies, you can create posts that resonate deeply with your audience and foster a thriving membership community.

Incorporating SEO Strategies for Discoverability

Incorporating effective SEO strategies is crucial for increasing the discoverability of your content on membership platforms. While creating engaging videos, writing compelling blog posts, or producing interactive content, you must also ensure that your audience can easily find your work. Start by conducting keyword research relevant to your niche. Use tools like Google Keyword Planner or Ubersuggest to identify keywords that resonate with your target audience. By strategically incorporating these keywords into your content, including titles, descriptions, and tags, you enhance your chances of ranking higher in search results, making it easier for potential subscribers to discover your offerings.

In addition to keywords, optimizing your video content is essential. Use catchy titles and detailed descriptions that include your chosen keywords. Ensure that your thumbnails are visually appealing and relevant to entice clicks. Incorporate closed captions and transcripts for your videos, as these not only improve accessibility but also provide search engines with additional content to index. The more relevant information you provide, the better your chances of appearing in search results. Remember that YouTube, a powerful search engine in its own right, can serve as a gateway to your membership platform, so treat it as an opportunity to drive traffic.

Another powerful SEO strategy is creating engaging blog posts that complement your video content. Writing articles that delve deeper into the topics you cover in your videos can attract organic traffic and provide valuable information for your audience. Include internal links to your videos and other related content within your posts. This not only enhances the user experience but also helps search engines understand the structure of your content. By consistently publishing insightful blog posts, you reinforce your authority in your niche and keep your audience engaged, encouraging them to subscribe to your membership offerings.

Social media is a powerful ally in boosting your discoverability as well. Promote your content across various platforms, ensuring to use relevant hashtags and keywords in your posts. Engaging with your audience through comments and messages can also strengthen your community and encourage more shares, further increasing your reach. Consider creating teaser content that leads back to your main offerings, whether it's a snippet of a podcast, a preview of a new video, or an engaging infographic. The more your followers interact with your content, the more likely it is to be seen by others outside your immediate circle.

Lastly, don't overlook the importance of analytics in your SEO strategy. Utilize the insights provided by platforms like Google Analytics and social media insights to understand what content resonates most with your audience. Track which keywords drive the most traffic and adjust your content strategy accordingly. By continually refining your approach based on data, you can enhance your discoverability and retention rates. Remember, building a successful membership platform takes time and effort, but with the right SEO strategies in place, you can significantly increase your chances of attracting and retaining members who are excited about what you create.

4

Podcasting for Membership Success

Developing Your Podcast Concept

Developing your podcast concept is a crucial step in establishing a successful presence on membership platforms. As content creators on platforms like OnlyFans, Patreon, and Fansly, you have the unique opportunity to connect with your audience on a more personal level through audio storytelling. Start by identifying your niche and the specific topics that resonate with your audience. Consider what you are passionate about and how that intersects with the interests of your subscribers. This alignment will not only make your podcast enjoyable for you to produce but will also keep your listeners engaged and eager for more.

Once you've pinpointed your niche, brainstorm potential themes and formats for your podcast. Will it be interview-based, where you invite fellow creators or experts to share their insights? Or maybe a solo format, where you dive deep into topics that matter most to your audience? Explore the possibility of integrating interactive elements, such as Q&A sessions or listener feedback segments. This not only fosters a sense of community but also encourages your subscribers to participate actively, enhancing their connection to your content.

Consider the frequency and length of your episodes as you develop your podcast concept. Consistency is key in building an audience, so think about how often you can realistically produce high-quality content. Whether it's weekly, biweekly, or monthly, ensure that your schedule aligns with your other commitments. Additionally, determine the ideal episode length. Shorter episodes may work well for quick updates or tips, while longer formats can allow for in-depth discussions. Tailor your approach to what you believe will best serve your audience's needs.

Branding is another essential aspect of your podcast concept. Choose a catchy and descriptive name that encapsulates the essence of your content. Create a visually appealing logo and cover art that reflects your style and resonates with your target audience. Establishing a strong brand identity will help your podcast stand out in a crowded market and make it easier for potential listeners to recognize and remember your show. Consistent branding across all platforms will reinforce your message and enhance your credibility as a content creator.

Finally, remember that your podcast is a reflection of your unique voice and creativity. Embrace the process of experimentation and iteration as you develop your concept. Don't hesitate to adjust your format or topics based on listener feedback and your own evolving interests. Building a successful podcast takes time and dedication, but with a well-defined concept that aligns with your audience's desires, you're well on your way to creating engaging content that fosters loyalty and community among your subscribers.

Recording and Editing Your Episodes

Recording and editing your episodes is a crucial step in creating engaging content that resonates with your audience on membership platforms. Whether you're an OnlyFans model, a Patreon user, or a content creator on Fansly, the quality of your videos and audio can significantly impact subscriber retention and engagement. To start, ensure you have the right equipment. Investing in a good microphone and camera is essential, as clear audio and sharp visuals can elevate your content and make your subscribers feel valued. Remember, your audience is paying for an experience, so delivering high-quality production is a way to show them that you care.

Once you have your equipment set up, it's time to consider your recording environment. Choose a quiet space with good lighting and minimal distractions. Natural light can work wonders, but if you're recording at night or in low light, consider using softbox lights or ring lights to create a flattering and professional look. Don't forget to eliminate background noise; closing windows, turning off fans, and using soundproofing materials can make a substantial difference in audio quality. The more effort you put into your recording environment, the better your content will resonate with your audience.

After recording, the editing process allows you to polish your content to perfection. Use editing software that suits your skill level and needs; options range from beginner-friendly tools like iMovie to more advanced programs like Adobe Premiere Pro. Focus on trimming any unnecessary content to keep your episodes concise and engaging. Including graphics, overlays, or subtitles can enhance viewer comprehension and retention. Remember, the goal of editing isn't just to cut out mistakes but to create a cohesive story that captivates your audience from start to finish.

Incorporating music and sound effects can also elevate your episodes, making them more dynamic and enjoyable. Choose royalty-free music that aligns with the tone of your content and complements your brand. Just be cautious not to let music overshadow your voice; it should enhance, not distract. Additionally, consider using sound bites or highlights from previous episodes to create a sense of continuity and encourage viewers to explore more of your content. Engaging your audience through thoughtful audio elements can significantly enhance their overall experience.

Finally, don't shy away from seeking feedback on your edited episodes. Share your content with trusted friends or fellow creators before going live. Their insights can help you identify areas for improvement that you might have missed. Remember, the journey of recording and editing is a learning process, so embrace constructive criticism and continue refining your skills. By prioritizing quality and engagement in your production process, you'll not only attract new subscribers but also foster a loyal community that appreciates your hard work and creativity.

Promoting Your Podcast to Attract Members

Promoting your podcast effectively is essential to attracting members to your membership platform. A well-crafted podcast can serve as an engaging entry point for potential subscribers, offering them a taste of the exclusive content you provide. Begin by identifying your target audience and tailoring your podcast's themes and discussions to resonate with their interests. This will not only help you build a loyal listener base but also foster a sense of community around your content. Consistency in publishing episodes will keep your audience engaged and eager for more, reinforcing their desire to subscribe to your membership offerings.

Leverage social media to amplify your podcast's reach. Utilize platforms like Instagram, Twitter, and TikTok to share snippets, quotes, and highlights from your episodes. Create visually appealing graphics or short video clips that encapsulate the essence of your discussions. This not only piques interest but also encourages sharing, expanding your audience organically. Engage directly with your followers by asking for their feedback or suggestions for future episodes, which can further foster community and make your audience feel valued.

Collaboration is another powerful strategy for promoting your podcast. Partner with other content creators or influencers in your niche to co-host episodes or participate in guest appearances. This not only exposes you to their audience but also enriches your content with diverse perspectives. When you collaborate, ensure that you promote these episodes across both your platforms, encouraging listeners to check out your membership site for more in-depth content and exclusive perks.

Email marketing remains a cornerstone for building and maintaining relationships with your audience. Use your podcast to encourage listeners to subscribe to your email list, offering exclusive content or behind-the-scenes insights as an incentive. Send regular newsletters that not only highlight new podcast episodes but also share valuable tips, upcoming events, and exclusive member-only content. This approach keeps your audience engaged and informed, making them more likely to transition from casual listeners to dedicated members.

Finally, be sure to encourage listener interaction. Invite your audience to submit questions, topics, or stories that they would like to hear discussed in future episodes. Incorporating listener feedback not only makes your content more relatable but also builds a deeper connection with your audience. By actively engaging with your listeners and making them feel like they are part of the conversation, you create a welcoming environment that encourages them to join your membership platform for even more interaction and exclusive content.

5

Interactive Content for Member Engagement

Types of Interactive Content to Create

Interactive content is a powerful way to engage your audience and strengthen your community on membership platforms. Among the various types of interactive content, polls and surveys stand out as essential tools for gauging audience preferences and collecting valuable feedback. By implementing these elements, you can create an ongoing dialogue with your subscribers, allowing them to feel more involved in your content creation process. This not only enhances their experience but also helps you tailor your offerings to meet their specific desires, ultimately boosting retention and satisfaction.

Quizzes and games are another fantastic avenue for interactive content. Creating fun and engaging quizzes relevant to your niche can not only entertain your audience but also provide insights into their interests and personalities. Whether it's a quiz to determine their favorite type of content or a fun trivia game related to your field, this type of content encourages participation and can be easily shared, expanding your reach. Consider integrating these quizzes into your social media or email campaigns, as they can drive traffic back to your main platform while simultaneously increasing engagement.

Live Q&A sessions present a unique opportunity for real-time interaction with your subscribers. By hosting these sessions, you can address questions, share insights, and foster a sense of community among your members. This format allows for a more personal connection, as fans can see and hear you while engaging directly. Promoting these events ahead of time and encouraging your audience to submit questions can set the stage for a lively and productive discussion, making them feel valued and heard.

Another exciting interactive content type is user-generated content. Encouraging your subscribers to create and share their own content related to your brand can lead to a vibrant community atmosphere. This approach not only showcases your audience's creativity but also builds a sense of ownership and loyalty to your platform. You might consider hosting contests or challenges that incentivize your fans to contribute their own videos, artwork, or stories, which can then be featured on your main channels, further driving engagement and connection.

Finally, incorporating interactive videos can significantly elevate your content strategy. These videos allow viewers to choose their own paths, making the viewing experience more immersive and personalized. By integrating clickable elements, such as links to additional content or options to vote on future topics, you can guide your audience deeper into your offerings while keeping them actively involved. This not only enhances viewer engagement but also encourages them to return for more, ensuring that your membership model remains dynamic and appealing.

Tools for Building Interactive Experiences

In the ever-evolving landscape of membership platforms, having the right tools at your disposal can significantly enhance the interactive experience for your audience. Whether you're an OnlyFans model, a Patreon creator, or a Fansly user, leveraging technology to engage your subscribers is crucial. Start by exploring a variety of content creation tools that can help you produce high-quality videos, podcasts, and written content. Platforms like Adobe Premiere Pro and Final Cut Pro offer advanced editing capabilities for video content, while tools such as Audacity and GarageBand are perfect for podcast production. Emphasizing quality and creativity not only captivates your audience but also fosters deeper connections.

Engagement doesn't stop at content creation; it's about creating a dynamic interaction with your audience. Consider integrating live streaming into your strategy. Platforms like Twitch and YouTube Live allow you to connect with your followers in real-time, providing an opportunity for immediate feedback and interaction. During live sessions, you can answer questions, take requests, or even involve your audience in the creative process. This level of engagement not only boosts viewer retention but also transforms passive subscribers into active participants, deepening their commitment to your content.

Incorporating interactive elements into your blog posts and social media can also significantly enhance member engagement. Tools like Typeform and SurveyMonkey can be used to create polls and quizzes that allow your audience to voice their opinions or preferences. This not only provides valuable feedback for your content creation but also makes your subscribers feel valued and heard. Additionally, platforms like Canva can help you design visually appealing graphics that complement your written content, making your posts more engaging and shareable.

Moreover, consider harnessing the power of email marketing to maintain and boost subscriber engagement. Tools such as Mailchimp and ConvertKit can help you automate your email campaigns, segment your audience, and personalize communications. Regular newsletters with exclusive content, behind-the-scenes insights, and interactive elements like Q&A sections can keep your audience eager for your next update. This consistent communication helps build a sense of community and loyalty among your subscribers, ensuring they remain invested in your membership offerings.

Finally, user-generated content can be an incredibly powerful tool for building community around your brand. Encourage your subscribers to share their experiences, creations, or feedback related to your content. Platforms like Instagram and TikTok can be used for this purpose, where fans can tag you in their posts, allowing you to showcase their contributions. Highlighting user-generated content not only promotes engagement but also creates a sense of belonging within your community. By utilizing these tools effectively, you can create a vibrant, interactive experience that not only attracts new members but also retains your existing audience, paving the way for long-term success on your chosen platform.

Measuring Engagement and Feedback

Measuring engagement and feedback is vital for any content creator operating on membership platforms. Understanding how your audience interacts with your content helps you refine your offerings and tailor experiences that resonate deeply with your subscribers. Whether you're an OnlyFans model, a Patreon user, or a content creator on Fansly, gathering data on engagement allows you to identify what works and what doesn't. This insight not only enhances your content strategy but also strengthens your bond with your audience, leading to increased retention and satisfaction.

One effective way to measure engagement is through analytics provided by the platforms themselves. Most membership sites offer built-in tools that track views, likes, comments, and shares. These metrics help you gauge the popularity of your content and understand viewer behavior. By analyzing this data, you can identify trends, such as peak engagement times, preferred content formats, and even demographic insights. This information empowers you to create more of what your audience loves, ensuring they remain excited and invested in your offerings.

In addition to quantitative data, qualitative feedback is equally important. Encourage your subscribers to share their thoughts through surveys, polls, and direct messages. This direct line of communication fosters a sense of community and makes your audience feel valued. When subscribers feel heard, they are more likely to engage actively with your content. Consider creating a monthly feedback session where you discuss what's working and what could be improved. This not only provides valuable insights but also strengthens the relationship between you and your audience.

Another powerful method to measure engagement is through interactive content. Live streams, Q&A sessions, and interactive polls can provide real-time feedback and engagement metrics. These formats not only encourage participation but also create a dynamic and lively atmosphere that keeps your audience coming back for more. By utilizing these interactive elements, you can gain immediate insights into your audience's preferences, making it easier to adapt your content strategy on the fly.

Finally, remember that engagement is an ongoing journey. Regularly revisiting and analyzing your metrics ensures that you stay aligned with your audience's needs and interests. As you grow and evolve as a content creator, so too will your audience's expectations. Keep the lines of communication open, stay adaptable, and embrace the feedback you receive. This proactive approach to measuring engagement and feedback will not only enhance your content offerings but also foster a thriving community around your brand, leading to long-term success in the membership landscape.

6

Designing Visual Content for Exclusive Members

The Importance of Branding

Branding is a crucial aspect of establishing yourself as a successful content creator on membership platforms. In an increasingly crowded digital marketplace, having a strong brand helps you stand out and communicate your unique value to your audience. It's not just about a logo or a catchy name; it's about building a cohesive identity that resonates with your subscribers. When you create a brand that reflects your personality, values, and the type of content you produce, you foster a sense of connection with your audience that can lead to loyalty and long-term engagement.

Your brand serves as the foundation for every piece of content you create, from videos and blog posts to podcasts and live streams. Consistency in branding helps your audience recognize and remember you across various platforms. This recognition builds trust, which is essential for encouraging subscribers to commit to your membership offerings. By presenting a unified visual style and voice, you enhance your credibility and make it easier for potential subscribers to understand what they can expect from your content.

Moreover, effective branding allows you to clearly define your niche and target audience. Whether you're an OnlyFans model, a Patreon artist, or a Fansly creator, identifying your unique selling proposition is vital. What makes your content different? What value do you provide that others do not? By honing in on these aspects, you not only attract the right audience but also cultivate a community that feels personally invested in your brand. This community is more likely to engage with your content, share it with others, and support you through subscriptions.

Branding also plays a significant role in your marketing strategies. A well-defined brand makes it easier to create promotional materials that resonate with your audience. Whether you're crafting social media posts, designing email campaigns, or developing interactive content, your brand identity should guide your messaging. This consistency not only reinforces your brand but also makes your marketing efforts more effective. When your audience sees your brand consistently represented, they are more likely to engage with your promotional content and convert into subscribers.

Finally, remember that branding is an evolving process. As you grow and your content evolves, so too can your brand. Embrace feedback from your community, experiment with new ideas, and be willing to adapt. Building a brand is not a one-time effort but a continuous journey that reflects your growth as a creator. By prioritizing your brand, you invest in your future success on membership platforms, ultimately leading to a more fulfilling and sustainable content creation career.

Creating Eye-Catching Graphics

Creating graphics that capture attention is essential for content creators on membership platforms like OnlyFans, Patreon, and Fansly. Eye-catching visuals can distinguish your content from the competition, drawing in potential subscribers and keeping existing members engaged. The right graphics can convey your brand's personality, enhance your storytelling, and create a more immersive experience for your audience. By investing time and effort into designing compelling visuals, you can significantly enhance the perceived value of your offerings.

Start by understanding the fundamentals of graphic design. Familiarize yourself with basic principles such as color theory, typography, and composition. These elements play a crucial role in how your graphics are perceived. Use contrasting colors to make important elements pop and choose fonts that reflect your brand's voice. Even if you're not a professional designer, there are countless online resources and tools available that can help you create polished graphics with ease. Platforms like Canva or Adobe Spark provide user-friendly interfaces and templates that can streamline your design process.

Incorporating your unique style into your graphics is key. Consider the themes and aesthetics that resonate with your audience and reflect your personality. Whether your niche is playful, edgy, or sophisticated, your visuals should evoke the same emotions and vibe. Use consistent branding elements across all your graphics, such as logos, color schemes, and imagery styles, to create a cohesive look. This not only enhances recognition but also builds a sense of trust and familiarity among your subscribers.

Another effective strategy is to leverage user-generated content. Encourage your members to share their experiences or creations related to your content, and showcase this material in your graphics. This approach not only fosters community engagement but also provides fresh, authentic visuals that resonate with your audience. Highlighting your subscribers' contributions can create a sense of belonging and encourage more interaction, ultimately enhancing member retention.

Finally, remember to test and iterate on your graphics. Monitor how different designs perform in terms of engagement and conversion rates. Utilize analytics to understand what resonates with your audience and refine your approach accordingly. By consistently updating and improving your graphics, you can stay relevant and maintain a vibrant presence in the dynamic landscape of membership platforms. Embrace the creative process, experiment with new ideas, and watch your content evolve into something truly captivating.

Using Visual Content to Tell Your Story

Using visual content to tell your story is an essential strategy for creators on membership platforms like OnlyFans, Patreon, and Fansly. Visuals can evoke emotions, create connections, and build a strong brand identity that resonates with your audience. By harnessing the power of photography, video, and graphics, you can share your unique journey and engage your subscribers on a deeper level. This subchapter will explore how to effectively utilize visual content to captivate your audience and foster a vibrant community.

First and foremost, authenticity is crucial in visual storytelling. Your audience wants to see the real you, so embrace your personality and showcase your experiences. Whether through behind-the-scenes footage, candid photos, or personal vlogs, sharing genuine moments helps to humanize your brand. This transparency not only builds trust but also encourages your subscribers to feel more connected to you. Highlight the creative process, share challenges, and celebrate victories with your audience—they will appreciate the vulnerability and commitment to sharing your story.

In addition to authenticity, consistency in your visual style can significantly enhance your storytelling efforts. Establishing a recognizable aesthetic—whether through color schemes, fonts, or imagery—creates a cohesive brand identity that subscribers can easily associate with you. Use tools like Canva or Adobe Spark to create templates for your visuals, ensuring that your content remains uniform across various platforms. This consistency helps reinforce your message and makes your brand memorable, which is essential for retaining subscribers and attracting new ones.

Moreover, consider the power of interactive visual content in engaging your audience. Live streaming, polls, and Q&A sessions not only allow you to share your story but also invite your subscribers to participate actively. These interactive formats foster a sense of community and give your audience a stake in your narrative. By incorporating their feedback and responses, you can tailor your content to better meet their interests and needs, ultimately enhancing their overall experience and increasing retention.

Lastly, remember to leverage user-generated content to enrich your storytelling. Encourage your subscribers to share their own experiences and interactions with your brand. This not only provides you with valuable insights but also creates a sense of belonging among your community. Featuring their contributions in your visual content—be it through testimonials, fan art, or shared moments—strengthens the bond between you and your audience. By celebrating their involvement, you not only enhance your narrative but also empower your subscribers to feel like an integral part of your journey.

7

Building Community Through Live Streaming

Choosing the Right Streaming Platform

Choosing the right streaming platform is a crucial step in your journey as a content creator on membership sites like OnlyFans, Patreon, and Fansly. With a plethora of options available, it's essential to consider what aligns best with your goals, audience, and content type. Each platform has its unique features tailored to different niches, so taking the time to research and evaluate them can make a significant difference in how effectively you engage with your audience and monetize your content.

When assessing streaming platforms, think about the type of content you intend to create. For instance, if your focus is on interactive live streams, look for platforms that support real-time engagement. Features like chat rooms, polls, and viewer interaction can enhance the streaming experience and foster a sense of community among your subscribers. Alternatively, if your primary content is pre-recorded videos or tutorials, platforms that offer robust video hosting capabilities and analytics can provide valuable insights into viewer behavior and preferences.

Another vital aspect to consider is the monetization options each platform provides. Some platforms allow you to set subscription tiers, while others may offer pay-per-view options or tips. Understanding these financial structures will help you choose a platform that not only meets your creative needs but also supports your income goals.

Additionally, consider whether the platform aligns with your brand identity and whether it allows for customization to create a cohesive look and feel that resonates with your audience.

User experience is another critical factor when selecting a streaming platform. A user-friendly interface can significantly impact how your audience interacts with your content. A platform that is easy to navigate encourages more engagement and keeps viewers coming back for more. Take the time to explore each platform's interface and consider testing them out to see which one feels right for both you and your audience. A seamless experience can lead to higher retention rates and a more robust community engagement.

Finally, don't underestimate the importance of community and support. Look for platforms that offer strong community features, such as forums or discussion groups, where you can connect with other creators and share experiences. Additionally, consider the type of customer support available, as having access to assistance can help you navigate any challenges that arise as you grow your membership base. By choosing a platform that supports you and fosters community, you can focus more on creating amazing content that resonates with your subscribers.

Engaging Your Audience in Real-Time

Engaging your audience in real-time is a powerful strategy that can significantly enhance the experience for your subscribers across membership platforms. As content creators, you have the unique opportunity to interact directly with your fans, transforming passive viewers into active participants. This interaction fosters a sense of community, making your subscribers feel valued and connected. Whether it's through live streaming, real-time polls, or interactive Q&A sessions, the immediacy of live engagement creates a dynamic environment where your audience can express their thoughts, ask questions, and share feedback instantly.

Live streaming has emerged as a crucial tool for creators on platforms like OnlyFans, Patreon, and Fansly. By hosting live sessions, you can showcase your personality and allow subscribers to see the real you, beyond the polished content they usually consume. Use these moments to connect on a personal level, share behind-the-scenes insights, and invite your audience into your creative process. This not only humanizes your brand but also encourages loyalty and retention as your subscribers feel they are part of your journey.

Incorporating interactive elements such as polls and Q&A sessions can significantly boost engagement. These tools allow your audience to influence the content you create, making them feel more invested in your work. For example, during a live stream, you can ask your audience what type of content they would like to see next or invite them to submit questions in real-time. This not only creates a more engaging experience but also provides you with valuable insights into your audience's preferences, helping you tailor your offerings to meet their desires.

Another effective strategy is to integrate user-generated content into your engagement efforts. Encourage your subscribers to share their own experiences related to your content, whether through comments, videos, or social media posts. Featuring their contributions in your live streams or exclusive member content acknowledges their participation and strengthens community ties. This not only makes your subscribers feel appreciated but also showcases the diverse perspectives within your audience, enriching the overall experience for everyone involved.

Finally, remember that consistency is key when engaging your audience in real-time. Establish a regular schedule for live events or interactive sessions so that your subscribers know when to tune in. Consistent engagement builds anticipation and creates a routine that can enhance loyalty. As you cultivate this real-time interaction, you'll not only deepen your connection with your audience but also create a vibrant community that supports and celebrates your creative endeavors. Embrace these opportunities to engage, and watch your membership thrive.

Strategies for Building a Loyal Community

Building a loyal community is essential for the success of any content creator on membership platforms like OnlyFans, Patreon, and Fansly. The first strategy to consider is creating a sense of belonging among your audience. This can be achieved by fostering open communication and encouraging member interaction. Engage with your subscribers through regular Q&A sessions, live chats, and community polls. Tailoring content based on their feedback not only makes them feel valued but also strengthens their connection to your brand. When members see that their opinions matter, they are more likely to stay committed and invested in your offerings.

Another effective strategy is to provide exclusive content that resonates with your audience's interests. Think about what makes your community unique and curate content that reflects their preferences. This could be behind-the-scenes access, early releases of videos, or personalized shout-outs. By offering something that they can't find elsewhere, you reinforce the value of their membership. Consistency is key; ensure that you regularly update your content to keep members excited and engaged. When subscribers feel they are receiving something special, it builds trust and loyalty.

Incorporating interactive elements into your content can significantly enhance community engagement. Consider hosting live streaming events, where members can participate in real-time. This not only allows for immediate feedback but also creates an atmosphere of camaraderie. You can also create challenges or contests that encourage user-generated content, prompting your audience to share their own experiences related to your niche. This active participation not only strengthens the community bond but also enriches your content library with fresh perspectives that can attract new members.

Utilizing email marketing effectively is another powerful strategy for retaining your community. Regular newsletters can keep your audience informed about upcoming events, new content, or special promotions. Make sure to personalize your messages to create a more intimate connection. Highlight community achievements, such as member spotlights or success stories, to reinforce a sense of collective identity. This approach not only keeps your community engaged but also fosters loyalty as members feel they are part of a larger journey, rather than just passive subscribers.

Lastly, always seek to evolve and adapt based on the changing needs of your community. Conduct regular surveys to gather feedback and identify areas for improvement. By demonstrating a willingness to listen and implement changes, you reinforce your commitment to your members. Creating a loyal community is not a one-time effort but an ongoing process of nurturing relationships. With dedication and genuine care for your audience, you can build a thriving community that supports your creative endeavors and enhances the overall experience for everyone involved.

8

Email Marketing for Retention

Crafting Compelling Email Campaigns

Crafting compelling email campaigns is essential for content creators on membership platforms like OnlyFans, Patreon, and Fansly. Your email list serves as a direct line of communication with your audience, allowing you to foster relationships and drive engagement. To create emails that resonate, it's crucial to personalize your messages. Use your subscribers' names and tailor content to reflect their interests. Segmenting your audience based on their preferences can help ensure that your emails are relevant, which increases the likelihood of engagement and conversion.

In addition to personalization, the value of your content cannot be overstated. Share exclusive insights, behind-the-scenes looks, or sneak peeks of upcoming content. Providing unique content that your subscribers can't find elsewhere will keep them looking forward to your emails. For instance, if you're a video content creator, consider sharing tips on video production or offering exclusive video clips. This not only adds value but also reinforces the idea that being a subscriber comes with unique benefits.

A strong call to action is a critical component of any successful email campaign. Whether you want your subscribers to watch a new video, join a live stream, or engage with a blog post, your call to action should be clear and compelling. Make it easy for them to take the next step by using buttons or links that stand out visually. The language you use matters too; phrases like "Join the community" or

"Don't miss out" create a sense of urgency and encourage immediate action.

Design plays a significant role in the effectiveness of your email campaigns. A visually appealing layout that reflects your brand can make a substantial difference in how your emails are received. Use images and graphics that resonate with your audience and complement your text. Consistent branding helps reinforce your identity and makes it easier for subscribers to recognize your emails in their inbox. Remember, a well-designed email not only captures attention but also enhances the overall reading experience.

Lastly, analyzing the performance of your email campaigns is crucial for ongoing improvement. Use metrics like open rates, click-through rates, and subscriber feedback to gauge what works and what doesn't. Experiment with different subject lines, content formats, and sending times to find the best combination for your audience. The insights gained from these analyses will empower you to refine your strategies and ensure your email campaigns remain compelling and effective, ultimately leading to greater membership retention and engagement.

Segmenting Your Audience for Better Results

Segmenting your audience is a powerful strategy that can significantly enhance your success on membership platforms like OnlyFans, Patreon, and Fansly. By understanding the diverse needs and preferences of your audience, you can create tailored content that resonates deeply with each segment. This targeted approach not only improves engagement but also fosters a strong sense of community among your subscribers, making them feel valued and understood. When you segment your audience effectively, you can deliver content that captivates, retains, and ultimately grows your membership base.

Begin by analyzing your existing audience data. Look for patterns in demographics, interests, and behaviors. Are there specific groups that respond better to certain types of content? For instance, some subscribers may be more interested in educational video content, while others may prefer behind-the-scenes glimpses or interactive experiences. Utilize tools provided by the membership platforms to gather insights, such as engagement rates on different types of posts or content formats. This data will help you identify distinct audience segments that you can cater to more effectively.

Once you have identified your segments, tailor your content strategy accordingly. For example, if you have a group of subscribers who are particularly interested in video production techniques, consider creating exclusive tutorials or behind-the-scenes videos that dive deeper into your creative process. For another segment that enjoys more interactive content, you might host live Q&A sessions or polls that encourage participation. By aligning your content with the specific interests of each segment, you not only boost engagement but also create a more personalized experience that keeps subscribers coming back for more.

Communication is key in keeping your audience informed about the segmented content you are offering. Use newsletters, social media updates, and announcements on your membership platform to highlight new content that caters to each segment. By doing this, you're not only promoting your work but also reinforcing the idea that each subscriber's interests are important to you. Encourage feedback and invite your audience to express their preferences, which will allow you to refine your segments and stay responsive to their evolving needs.

Ultimately, segmenting your audience is about building stronger relationships and fostering loyalty. When members feel that their unique needs are being met, they are more likely to engage with your content and remain subscribed for the long term. By investing the time to understand and cater to the diverse segments within your audience, you are setting the stage for sustainable growth and success on membership platforms. Embrace this strategy, and watch your community flourish as you create content that truly resonates with each individual member.

Analyzing Metrics to Improve Future Campaigns

Analyzing metrics is a powerful tool that can significantly enhance the effectiveness of your future campaigns on membership platforms. For content creators, understanding the data behind your audience's engagement can illuminate which types of content resonate most with your subscribers. This insight is not just about numbers; it's about understanding your community better. By diving into analytics, you can uncover patterns and preferences that inform your content strategy, ensuring that each video, blog post, or podcast episode speaks directly to your audience's interests.

When you begin analyzing your metrics, start with the basics: views, likes, shares, and comments. These initial indicators provide a snapshot of how your content is performing. However, don't stop there. Delve deeper into audience retention rates to see how long viewers engage with your videos or the drop-off points in your podcasts. Identifying these moments can reveal what captivates your audience and what might need tweaking. The goal is to create content that not only attracts but also holds their attention, fostering a deeper connection with your members.

Engagement metrics can guide your content creation process in real-time. If you notice a spike in interaction with a particular topic, consider producing more content along those lines. Alternatively, if certain formats, such as live streams or interactive posts, yield higher engagement, it may be time to pivot your strategy. Experimentation is key; don't hesitate to try new ideas based on the data you collect. By continuously testing and adapting, you can keep your content fresh and aligned with your members' evolving preferences.

Feedback from your audience is another essential metric that should not be overlooked. Encourage your subscribers to share their thoughts on your content through polls, surveys, or direct messages. This qualitative data complements the quantitative metrics, providing context and insights that numbers alone cannot convey. Engaging your community in this way not only makes them feel valued but also gives you direct input on what they want to see more of, creating a collaborative atmosphere that enhances loyalty and retention.

In summary, analyzing metrics is an ongoing journey that empowers you as a creator. By leveraging both quantitative and qualitative data, you can craft a more compelling content strategy that resonates with your audience. Remember, each piece of feedback or data point is an opportunity to refine your approach, ensuring that you remain connected with your members and continuously deliver the valuable content they seek. Embrace this analytical mindset, and watch your membership campaigns flourish as you build a vibrant, engaged community.

9

Course Creation for Membership Learning

Identifying Topics That Resonate

Identifying topics that resonate with your audience is crucial for success on membership platforms like OnlyFans, Patreon, and Fansly. It all begins with understanding the interests, desires, and pain points of your subscribers. Take time to research your target audience by analyzing trends within your niche and examining what content performs well on social media and other platforms.

Engage with your community through polls, Q&As, and direct messages to gain insights into their preferences. This feedback can guide your content creation process and ensure you're delivering what your members truly want.

Once you gather insights from your audience, focus on creating content that aligns with their interests while staying true to your unique voice. Authenticity is key; your subscribers are drawn to you for a reason, and they appreciate content that reflects your personality and style. Consider blending popular topics within your niche with your personal experiences, stories, or perspectives. This fusion not only keeps your content fresh and relatable but also fosters a deeper connection with your audience, making them feel more invested in your journey.

Exploring different content formats can also help you identify what resonates best. Video content can be powerful, as it allows for personal interaction and engagement. However, don't overlook the potential of blogs, podcasts, and live streams. Experiment with various types of content to see what your audience engages with the most. Analyzing the performance of these formats will provide invaluable data that can refine your approach and highlight the topics that drive the most interaction and subscription growth.

Additionally, consider leveraging trends and current events to create timely and relevant content. This not only positions you as an informed creator but also encourages members to engage with your content more actively. By staying attuned to what's happening in your niche and the broader world, you can create content that sparks conversation and encourages sharing. This strategy not only boosts your visibility but also fosters a sense of community among your members, as they feel they are part of a larger dialogue.

Finally, don't hesitate to revisit and adapt your topics over time. Audience interests can evolve, and being flexible in your content strategy will keep your membership thriving. Regularly solicit feedback from your subscribers and be open to incorporating new ideas and suggestions into your content plan. By constantly identifying and refining topics that resonate, you will not only enhance member satisfaction but also create a dynamic and engaging platform that fosters long-term loyalty and retention.

Structuring Your Course for Maximum Value

When structuring your course for maximum value, it's essential to start with a clear understanding of your audience and their needs. As content creators on platforms like OnlyFans, Patreon, and Fansly, you have the unique opportunity to cater directly to your subscribers' interests and desires. Begin by conducting surveys or engaging with your community to gather insights about what they would like to learn. This information will help you tailor your course content to ensure it resonates deeply with your members, making them feel valued and understood.

Next, consider breaking your course into manageable modules or sections. This approach not only makes the content more digestible but also allows your members to progress at their own pace. Each module should focus on a specific topic or skill, such as video production techniques, writing engaging blog posts, or strategies for effective email marketing. By providing a structured format, you empower your members to follow along easily and keep them motivated as they witness their progress.

Incorporating interactive elements into your course can dramatically enhance member engagement. Think about integrating quizzes, discussion boards, or live Q&A sessions where your subscribers can interact with you and each other. This not only fosters a sense of community but also encourages deeper learning. Interactive content can make your course feel more dynamic and less transactional, which is crucial for maintaining long-term relationships with your subscribers.

Visual design plays a vital role in how your course is perceived and experienced. Investing in high-quality visuals and easy-to-navigate layouts can elevate the overall user experience. Use engaging graphics, infographics, and videos to break up text-heavy sections and maintain interest. Remember, your course is not just about delivering information; it's about creating an immersive experience that keeps your members coming back for more.

Finally, don't underestimate the power of feedback and iteration. Encourage your members to share their thoughts on your course's structure and content, and be open to making adjustments based on their input. This not only shows that you value their opinions but also enhances the course's relevance over time. By continuously refining your offering, you can ensure that your course remains a valuable resource for your community, ultimately leading to greater retention and satisfaction among your subscribers.

Delivering Your Course Effectively

Delivering your course effectively is pivotal in engaging your audience and ensuring they gain maximum value from your content. Start by understanding your unique audience—OnlyFans models, Patreon users, Fansly users, and other content creators are seeking not just information but also inspiration and practical tools to elevate their membership platforms. Tailor your course materials to address the specific challenges and aspirations of your niche. This targeted approach helps establish a connection and fosters trust, encouraging members to invest their time and resources into your offerings.

Creating a dynamic learning experience requires careful planning and execution. Utilize a mix of video, audio, and visual materials to cater to different learning styles. For instance, in video content production, demonstrate techniques that content creators can easily replicate, such as lighting setups or editing tips. Incorporate interactive elements like quizzes or polls to reinforce learning and keep participants engaged. Additionally, consider live Q&A sessions where participants can seek clarification and share their experiences. This interactivity not only enhances comprehension but also builds a sense of community among your members.

One of the key components of delivering an effective course is consistent communication. Utilize email marketing strategies to keep your audience informed about upcoming sessions, new materials, and exclusive content. Regular newsletters can provide valuable insights, tips, and updates that reinforce the learning experience. Encourage participants to share their progress and experiences through social media or dedicated forums, fostering a collaborative environment. This two-way communication not only enhances retention but also empowers your members to take ownership of their learning journey.

Remember, the delivery of your course should also reflect your personality and passion for the subject matter. Use storytelling techniques to share personal anecdotes or case studies that illustrate the concepts you teach. This not only makes your content more relatable but also inspires your audience to apply what they learn in their own content creation efforts. Your enthusiasm will resonate with participants, encouraging them to engage more deeply with the course material and implement what they learn effectively.

Finally, gather feedback from your members to continuously improve your course offerings. Create opportunities for participants to share their thoughts on the content, delivery, and overall experience. This feedback loop is invaluable for refining your materials and ensuring that you meet the evolving needs of your audience. By committing to delivering your course effectively, you empower your members not only to thrive on their respective platforms but also to build thriving communities that enrich the subscription experience for all involved.

10

Social Media Strategies for Promotion

Choosing the Right Platforms for Your Audience

Choosing the right platforms for your audience is crucial for maximizing your content's reach and ensuring that you connect with your ideal subscribers. Each membership platform, whether it's OnlyFans, Patreon, or Fansly, offers unique features and caters to different demographics. Understanding these nuances allows you to tailor your content strategy effectively. Start by analyzing the preferences and behaviors of your target audience. Are they more likely to engage with visual content, audio podcasts, or written materials? By aligning your content format with their interests, you can foster deeper connections and encourage ongoing subscription.

When it comes to video content production, consider the strengths of each platform. For instance, OnlyFans is often associated with adult content, but it also has a growing community of creators producing lifestyle and fitness videos. Patreon, on the other hand, is known for its diverse range of creative outputs, from tutorials to exclusive behind-the-scenes footage. Evaluate where your content fits best and think about how you can leverage the platform's tools to enhance viewer engagement. Experiment with live streaming or interactive video sessions to create a more immersive experience for your subscribers.

Writing engaging blog posts is another powerful way to connect with your audience. Platforms like Patreon allow you to publish written content alongside your videos, creating a multi-dimensional experience. Blogs can serve as a space for deeper storytelling, sharing personal insights, or providing additional value related to your video content. Use this opportunity to foster a sense of community by encouraging comments and discussions. Engaging your audience through thoughtful writing not only keeps them invested but also positions you as a trusted voice in your niche.

Social media plays a pivotal role in promoting your membership content. Each platform—be it Instagram, Twitter, or TikTok—has its own strengths when it comes to reaching potential subscribers. Tailor your promotional strategies based on where your audience spends their time online. Use visually appealing snippets from your videos, engaging posts about your blog entries, or exciting announcements about live streams to draw in new members. Remember, consistency is key; maintaining a regular presence will keep your audience informed and eager to engage with your content.

Lastly, consider user-generated content strategies to enhance member engagement. Encourage your subscribers to share their experiences with your content, whether through testimonials, feedback, or even collaborative projects. This not only builds a sense of community but also provides you with fresh ideas and perspectives that can inform your future content. By choosing the right platforms and adopting a multi-faceted approach to your content creation, you can cultivate a loyal audience that feels valued and connected to your brand. Embrace the journey, and let your creativity shine as you build a thriving membership community.

Creating Shareable Content

Creating shareable content is essential for maximizing your reach and enhancing engagement on membership platforms. As content creators on sites like OnlyFans, Patreon, and Fansly, you have a unique opportunity to connect with your audience in meaningful ways. The first step to creating shareable content is understanding your audience's interests and preferences. By tapping into the themes and topics that resonate with them, you can produce material that not only entertains but also encourages your subscribers to share your work with their networks.

One effective strategy for generating shareable content is to leverage current trends and popular culture. This could involve creating videos that incorporate trending challenges, memes, or hot topics within your niche. By aligning your content with what's currently capturing attention, you not only increase your chances of going viral but also position yourself as a relevant and timely creator. Think about how you can put your unique spin on these trends to showcase your personality and signature style.

Another powerful approach is to encourage interactivity within your content. Engaging your audience through polls, Q&A sessions, or challenges can prompt them to share your content as they become more invested in your community. For example, you might create a challenge that invites your subscribers to post their results on social media, tagging you in the process. This not only broadens your reach but also fosters a sense of belonging among your members, making them feel like active participants rather than passive viewers.

Visual appeal plays a crucial role in shareability, particularly in the realm of social media. High-quality images, eye-catching thumbnails, and aesthetically pleasing graphics can draw attention and entice viewers to click and share. Consider investing time in learning design tools or collaborating with graphic designers to ensure that your visuals reflect the quality of your content. Remember, the more attractive your content looks, the more likely it is to be shared by your audience.

Finally, don't underestimate the power of storytelling. Content that tells a compelling story tends to resonate more deeply with audiences, increasing the likelihood of sharing. Whether it's through a blog post, a video narrative, or a podcast episode, weaving personal anecdotes or relatable experiences into your content can create a connection that encourages sharing. Aim to create content that not only informs but also inspires, uplifts, and entertains, and you will find your work being shared far beyond your immediate community.

Utilizing Ads to Expand Your Reach

Utilizing ads effectively can be a game-changer for OnlyFans models, Patreon users, Fansly users, and other content creators aiming to expand their reach. The digital landscape offers a plethora of advertising options, from social media ads to search engine marketing, each providing a unique pathway to attract new subscribers. By strategically investing in ads, you can amplify your presence, draw in potential fans, and ultimately increase your revenue. Understanding the nuances of each platform allows you to tailor your approach, ensuring that your advertising efforts resonate with your target audience.

One of the most effective ways to utilize ads is through social media platforms, where engagement levels are high, and audience targeting is precise. Platforms like Instagram, Facebook, and TikTok allow you to create visually appealing ads that showcase your content, whether it's enticing snippets of your videos, behind-the-scenes glimpses of your creative process, or testimonials from satisfied subscribers. By crafting compelling ad copy and utilizing eye-catching visuals, you can capture the attention of potential members who may not yet be aware of the value you offer. Remember, the goal is to make a memorable first impression that encourages clicks and conversions.

In addition to social media, search engine marketing can play a pivotal role in expanding your reach. By optimizing your ads with relevant keywords, you can position yourself in front of users actively searching for content like yours. Google Ads and similar platforms allow you to target specific demographics, ensuring your ads reach individuals who are most likely to engage with your offerings. Don't shy away from experimenting with different ad formats, such as video ads or display ads, to see what resonates best with your audience. Analyzing the performance of these ads can provide valuable insights that inform your future marketing strategies.

Collaborating with other creators can also amplify your advertising efforts. Partnering with fellow content creators within your niche allows you to tap into their audience while providing them with value in return. Cross-promotional ads can introduce your content to new potential fans who may appreciate your unique offerings. This synergistic approach not only expands your reach but fosters a sense of community among creators, enhancing overall engagement across platforms. Building relationships with other creators can lead to exciting collaborative projects that further enrich your content and appeal to your audience.

Lastly, don't overlook the power of retargeting ads to engage those who have already shown interest in your content. These ads remind past visitors of what they're missing and encourage them to return or subscribe. Through enticing offers or exclusive content previews, retargeting ads can convert window-shoppers into loyal subscribers. By continuously refining your ad strategy based on performance metrics and audience feedback, you can create a dynamic marketing approach that evolves with your growing brand. Embrace the potential of ads to not only expand your reach but to build lasting connections with your audience.

11

User-Generated Content for Engagement

Encouraging Members to Create Content

Encouraging your members to create content can significantly enhance the richness of your platform and foster a vibrant community. As a creator, you understand the value of diverse perspectives and varied content types. By inviting your members to share their own creations, you not only empower them but also create an environment where everyone feels valued and connected. This collaborative spirit encourages retention and engagement, as members see their contributions celebrated within the community.

One effective way to motivate your members is by showcasing member-generated content prominently. This can be done through features like "Member of the Month" or dedicated sections on your platform where their work is highlighted. When members see their peers recognized, it ignites a sense of pride and encourages them to contribute their own content. Additionally, consider hosting contests or challenges that incentivize creativity. Offering rewards, such as exclusive access or shout-outs, can create excitement and increase participation.

Engagement is also fostered through clear communication about the types of content you are looking for. Providing guidelines and examples can help members feel more confident in their ability to contribute. Share success stories from other members to illustrate how their content has positively impacted the community. This not only provides inspiration but also reassures potential contributors that their efforts will be appreciated and valued, making them more likely to participate.

Creating a supportive environment is crucial. Encourage feedback and interaction among members regarding their content. Establishing forums or discussion threads where creators can seek advice or collaborate can lead to a thriving ecosystem of creativity. By fostering relationships among members, you cultivate a sense of belonging, making them more inclined to share their creative efforts. Regularly engage with their content through comments or shares to show appreciation for their contributions.

Lastly, leverage different content formats to engage a broader audience. Encourage members to explore various mediums, such as video, podcasts, or written blogs, allowing them to express themselves in ways that resonate with them. Providing tools or resources for content creation can also remove barriers and empower members to share their work. By promoting a culture of creativity and collaboration, you will not only enrich your platform but also build a strong, engaged community that thrives on mutual support and shared experiences.

Showcasing User Contributions

Showcasing user contributions is a powerful strategy that can elevate the presence of your membership platform and foster a vibrant community. When you highlight the work and creativity of your subscribers, you not only validate their efforts but also encourage others to engage more deeply. This practice transforms your platform into a collaborative space where members feel valued and inspired to contribute, leading to a richer content ecosystem that benefits everyone involved.

Incorporating user-generated content into your offerings can take many forms, from featuring fan art and testimonials to sharing video clips created by your supporters. For instance, if you're an OnlyFans model, consider showcasing artistic interpretations of your work or curated content from fans who have been inspired by you. This not only honors their creativity but also strengthens the connection between you and your audience. By giving your members a spotlight, you create an inclusive environment where everyone feels like a part of the journey.

Engaging your community through contests or challenges can also stimulate user contributions. Encourage your subscribers to create content based on themes or prompts you provide, and reward the best submissions with features on your social media or even exclusive perks. This approach not only generates excitement but also allows your creators to showcase their talents and creativity. As members see their contributions recognized, they are more likely to engage regularly, creating a cycle of encouragement and creativity that enhances the overall experience on your platform.

Furthermore, integrating user contributions into your marketing strategies can be a game-changer. When you share user-generated content across your social media channels, it acts as authentic testimonials that can attract new members. Potential subscribers are drawn to communities that actively celebrate and uplift their members. Highlighting these contributions not only showcases the talent within your community but also positions your platform as one that values and nurtures creativity, making it more appealing to newcomers.

Finally, fostering a culture of appreciation and recognition for user contributions can significantly impact member retention. Regularly acknowledging and celebrating the work of your subscribers through newsletters, social media shout-outs, or even dedicated segments in your podcasts or live streams can create a loyal and engaged community. When members see that their efforts are appreciated, they are more likely to remain active and committed to your platform, contributing to its growth and vibrancy. By showcasing user contributions, you create a dynamic where everyone can thrive together, enriching the content landscape for all involved.

Leveraging UGC for Community Building

User-generated content (UGC) is a powerful tool for fostering community among your subscribers on membership platforms. By encouraging your fans to contribute their own content, you not only enhance engagement but also create a sense of belonging that can significantly boost retention. This type of content can take many forms, including photos, videos, testimonials, or even written stories that reflect their experiences with your brand. By showcasing UGC, you demonstrate that you value your community's input, which creates a two-way relationship that enhances loyalty.

To effectively leverage UGC, start by creating campaigns or prompts that encourage your subscribers to share their content. For instance, consider running contests where fans submit their best photos or videos related to your niche. This not only incentivizes participation but also generates a buzz around your content. Promote these campaigns across your social media and other channels, making it easy for fans to participate. When you recognize and reward contributions, you elevate the sense of community, as members feel seen and appreciated for their efforts.

Once you've collected UGC, share it on your platforms in a way that encourages further interaction. Highlighting fan content in your newsletters, social media, or even in your main video content can motivate others to participate as well. This visibility fosters a culture of sharing and collaboration within your community. Additionally, by tagging and acknowledging contributors, you strengthen relationships and encourage more fans to engage, knowing their efforts could be spotlighted.

Engaging with UGC can also provide you with valuable insights into your audience's preferences and interests. By analyzing what types of content resonate most with your community, you can tailor your future offerings to better meet their needs. This not only enhances your content strategy but also shows your audience that you are listening and responding to their desires, further solidifying their commitment to your brand.

Finally, remember that UGC is not just about content; it's about building a vibrant community. Encourage discussions around the shared content, create spaces for fans to connect, and facilitate interactions that go beyond just liking or commenting. Through live streams, Q&A sessions, or exclusive member forums, you can deepen these connections. By actively fostering a community where your fans feel valued and engaged, you create an environment that thrives on collaboration, ultimately leading to greater membership success.

Want to Learn More from Big Daddy Dakota? Check out the following pages:

OnlyFans (Not That Kind of Page, We Don't Pass Judgement): https://onlyfans.com/bigdaddydakota96